Fun Thi Retirement

Looking for ways to make your retirement enjoyable and meaningful without breaking the bank? Look no further! We've got a list of affordable activities that will not only bring fun into your life, but also enrich it in a fulfilling way. Whether you're looking to explore new hobbies, volunteer in your community, or travel to new places, we've got you covered. So why wait? Start living your best retirement life today!

MIKE DAVIDS

INTRODUCTION

Congratulations on reaching this amazing milestone in your life! You have overcome so many challenges and have made a positive impact on those around you through your hard work and dedication. Now, it's time to embrace the joys of retirement and spend your days doing the things that truly make you happy. However, with so many possibilities to consider, it's understandable to feel overwhelmed. That's why we're here to help you find activities that align with your passions and interests. By doing what you love, you can break away from old habits and routines that no longer serve you, and create a new path that brings you joy and fulfillment. Writing down your goals and desires can help you gain clarity and commit to them, ensuring that you make the most of this exciting new chapter in your life. Let's explore all the possibilities together and make your retirement years truly unforgettable!

HOW TO USE THIS BOOK

Congratulations on embarking on this exciting journey towards creating a fulfilling and meaningful retirement! This book will guide you through the process of reflecting on your life, your skills, and your passions to create a customized bucket list that is deeply focused on enriching your life and fulfilling your deepest desires. The themed categories in this book, such as expanding your social circle, investigating religion and spirituality, and daring to live dangerously, will inspire you with a variety of ideas that will push you out of your comfort zone and help you make the most of your retirement. This is your opportunity to make your "third act" the best it can possibly be! As you explore the ideas in this book, take the time to consider what feels right for you. After all, your retirement plans should be as unique as you are. You can also add your own entries and go at your own pace. Whether you choose to focus on creativity, playfulness, travel, or anything in between, the most important rule is to have fun doing it! Let's create a retirement that is tailored to your interests and passions, and that brings you joy and fulfillment in this exciting new chapter of your life.

IMPORTANT QUESTIONS ABOUT YOU

Before impulsively adding items to your bucket list, it's important to pause and reflect on your past experiences, what you enjoyed and didn't enjoy, your existing skills and those you'd like to develop. Use this self-discovery to inform what you might find fulfilling in the future, rather than feeling pressure to conform to societal expectations of retirement activities like golfing, lawn bowling, or quilting. If those activities don't excite you, it's perfectly fine to explore other options.

To help you brainstorm, consider these nine questions:

1. WHAT SPARKS MY PASSION?

Is spending time with your grandkids the highlight of your day? Have you always had a love for woodworking, but haven't had the chance to pursue it lately? Does the thought of ice skating, watching motorsports, or making homemade pasta excite you? Consider your long-standing interests that you've yet to explore fully. Make a list of your top five passions.

2. WHAT ARE MY CURRENT SKILLS AND INTERESTS?

Over the years, you've likely developed valuable skills that you may not even realize are skills. Are you an exceptional communicator? Can you soothe a crying child with ease? Do animals gravitate towards you and follow your lead? Are you a natural at making new friends and putting people at ease? Perhaps you have a talent for making others laugh, managing finances, or impressing others with your knowledge of history. Take a moment to reflect on your accomplishments and the skills you've honed throughout your life, whether intentionally or by chance. Recognizing these strengths can boost your confidence and happiness. Who knows, perhaps you can leverage these skills to volunteer for a cause you care about. List three skills that you've developed over time.

3. WHAT AM I NOT SKILLED AT OR DISLIKE DOING CURRENTLY?

While it's important to identify your strengths and passions, it's equally important to acknowledge what you don't enjoy doing or what you struggle to master. For instance, if you dread washing dishes, investing in a dishwasher could make your life happier. Or perhaps you despise giving speeches, even though you're an excellent public speaker.

It's perfectly fine to dislike certain activities, no matter how good you are at them. You might find relief by intentionally letting go of these activities and focusing on what brings you joy. Take note of activities you want to release from your life to gain clarity moving forward.

Note: Gaining clarity on what you want to move on from doesn't mean being selfish with your time or neglecting those who rely on you.

4. HOW DO I ENVISION SPENDING MY RETIREMENT YEARS?

Consider the endless possibilities of how you could spend your retirement years. Do you picture yourself spending more time with family and friends? Traveling to new places or revisiting old favorites? Pursuing a new hobby or revisiting a long-standing passion? Volunteering for a cause you care about? It's important to identify what brings you the most joy and fulfillment. Envision how you want to spend your time and what activities will bring you the most happiness. Write down your thoughts to help clarify your vision for your retirement years.

5. WHAT LIFESTYLE OR COMMITMENTS DO I WANT TO REDUCE OR STOP ENTIRELY?

Consider your current lifestyle and commitments. Are there any activities or commitments that no longer bring you joy or fulfillment? Are there any that you want to reduce or stop participating in entirely? Perhaps you want to spend less time on social media or watching television, or maybe you want to step down from a leadership role in a volunteer organization. It's essential to identify what activities or commitments are no longer serving you and what you want to let go of to make room for new experiences. Write down any commitments or lifestyle habits that you want to reduce or eliminate entirely.

_____

_____

_____

_____

6. WHAT CURRENT COMMITMENTS OR LIFESTYLE HABITS DO I WANT TO REDUCE OR ELIMINATE?

---

7. WHAT CURRENT COMMITMENTS DO I WANT TO EMBRACE AND DO MORE OF IN MY RETIREMENT?

---

8. WHAT CURRENT COMMITMENTS DO I WANT TO SCALE BACK OR MOVE ON FROM?

Take a moment to reflect on your current commitments and activities. Are there any that you want to scale back or move on from, even if they have brought you joy in the past? Perhaps you want to reduce your work hours or step down from a leadership position in a volunteer organization. It's important to identify what commitments or activities you may want to let go of to make room for new experiences in your retirement years. Write down any commitments or activities that you want to scale back or move on from.

_____

_____

_____

9. WHAT DOES AN IDEAL DAY IN RETIREMENT LOOK LIKE?

Envision your ideal day in retirement. What activities would you like to do? How would you like to spend your time? Maybe you want to start your day with a cup of coffee and a good book, followed by a morning walk or workout.

Perhaps you want to spend the afternoon gardening or pursuing a creative hobby. Consider what brings you joy and fulfillment and how you want to spend your time. Write down your vision for your ideal day in retirement to help guide your planning and decision-making.

LET'S START

Let's start with some easy, fun ideas that I bet you've already thought about in the lead-up to your well-earned extended vacation.

BOOKS TO READ

Have you always meant to read the classics, like "The Great Gatsby" or "War and Peace"? How about everything ever by an author, like Jane Austen or Stephen King? Did you love Marvel comics as a kid, or would you like to give biographies or science fiction a try? Create a list of the top 20 books you'd like to read.

MOVIES TO SEE

Are you looking for some great movie recommendations to add to your watchlist? Perhaps you've been wanting to indulge in the legendary "The Corleone Family" trilogy, or immerse yourself in the timeless musicals of "Williams and Hammerstein". If you're a fan of suspense, you might want to check out the iconic films of "Alexandra Hitchcock", or if you prefer explosive action, "Matthew Bay's" impressive collection of work. Jot down your list of must-see movies here and get ready for some unforgettable cinematic experiences!

RECIPES TO COOK

Do you have any recipes that have proven to be a challenge for you in the past? Or are there any exciting cuisines you've never tried before and want

Have you always meant to read the classics, like "The Great Gatsby" or "War and Peace"? How about everything ever by an author, like Jane Austen or Stephen King? Did you love Marvel comics as a kid, or would you like to give biographies or science fiction a try? Create a list of the top 20 books you'd like to read.

TV SHOWS TO WATCH

Do you miss the TV shows you used to love watching during your youth? Or are there some shows that you've been meaning to watch but haven't had the chance to yet? Why not ask your friends and family for their favorite film and TV recommendations? This way, you can discover what they enjoy and even have some great conversations about it! List your list of TV shows to binge-watch here.

_____

_____

_____

EXCITING PURSUITS TO TRY

Have you ever considered trampolining, screen print-
ing, or even agility training with your furry friend?
Don't limit yourself to the usual hobbies and
activities - let your curiosity lead the way! Jot down
your list of new pursuits to try here and get ready for
some fun and adventure.

_____

_____

_____

GARDENING

Doing some work in the garden is a great way to stay active during your golden years. While you may not think of it as such, gardening is an effective low-impact workout that uses muscles from head to toe, plus it gives you the added benefit of being outside.

Studies have shown that gardening for just half an hour a day is a great way for seniors to meet their body's physical activity needs. This activity can help reduce your blood pressure, improve your mood, increase your body's levels of vitamin D, and help decrease stress.

Many neighborhoods or counties also have garden clubs where people who enjoy gardening come together. Garden clubs do various things such as hosting flower shows and giving garden tutorials for projects that aim at bettering the landscape of your community. Garden clubs help people share knowledge, meet other gardening enthusiasts, and learn new things about the craft.

WATCH THE SUNSET OR SUNRISE

There are sunsets and sunrises every single day. And they're free to watch. So make sure you don't miss many of them. They are breathtaking, and it has been proven that watching the sunrise or sunset gives you a better sense of gratitude for the earth.

It's because when you are caught up in the natural beauty of a sunset or sunrise, you rid yourself of any distractions. And you feel higher levels of satisfaction and gratitude for what's happening in front of you. So, a great way to start or end your retirement day.

LISTEN TO PODCATS

A podcast is the modern version of a radio show, but it's recorded so you can listen to it anytime you want. There are a lot of podcasts out there that are inspiring and interesting listening to. You can look for podcasts related to retirement, your hobby, or other topics in life.

DAY TRIPS TO TAKE

Why go through the hassle of planning and organizing a day trip when you can simply join a pre-arranged tour? There are so many fantastic options available, from winery tours to antiques tours, art museum tours, coastal road trips, and even horseback riding tours. By joining one of these tours, you can save time and effort since all the planning has been taken care of for you. Plus, you'll have the opportunity to meet new people who share your passions and interests. So why not take the easy route and enjoy a stress-free adventure on your next day trip?

INTERNATIONAL DESTINATIONS TO EXPERIENCE

The world is full of incredible destinations waiting to be explored, each with its unique charm and beauty. From the ancient pyramids of Egypt to the majestic wilderness of Africa and the picturesque castles and hills of Switzerland, the options are endless. So, where would you like to go? And how would you like to get there? Would you prefer a luxurious cruise or a scenic train ride? Maybe you're more interested in renting an RV, staying in a cozy tiny house, or even trying out a houseboat.

The possibilities are endless! So, why not make a list of your dream travel destinations and experiences and start planning your next unforgettable adventure?

DISCOVER THE HIDDEN GEMS IN YOUR NEIGHBORHOOD

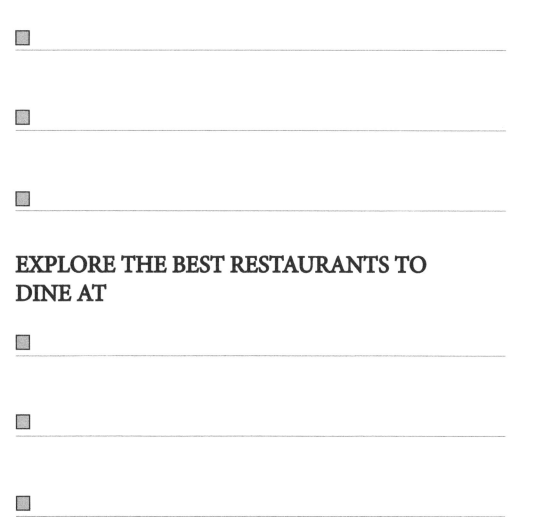

- ☐ _____

- ☐ _____

- ☐ _____

EXPLORE THE BEST RESTAURANTS TO DINE AT

- ☐ _____

- ☐ _____

- ☐ _____

UNCOVER THE TOP FESTIVALS AND EVENTS IN YOUR REGION.

☐ _____

☐ _____

☐ _____

VISIT FAMILY.

Spending time with family is what most people are looking forward to retirement. And especially if your family lives close by you can visit them as often as you like. Make it a priority in retirement to spend as much time with your loved ones as you can.

THE PEOPLE YOU SHOULD INVEST YOUR TIME IN.

Life is busy, and sometimes we don't get to spend as much time as we'd like with the people we care about. Take a moment to think about the individuals who have brought joy and positivity to your life but whom you haven't seen in a while. Maybe it's an old friend, a family member, or a colleague you used to work closely with.

Whatever the case may be, jot down their names and consider reaching out to them to reconnect. Who knows, they may feel the same way and be excited to catch up with you too! So don't hesitate, make plans to spend more time with the people who matter to you and create new memories together.

WHO TO MINIMIZE TIME SPENT WITH.

As we go through life, we meet many different people, and not all of them are meant to stay in our lives forever. If there are individuals who drain your energy, bring you down, or take up too much of your time and emotional space, it may be time to consider spending less time with them. Take a moment to reflect on the people in your life and identify those who may fall into this category. Write down their names and silently thank them for the memories you shared together.

Then, wish them well and let them go mentally to make room for new, positive relationships that bring fulfillment to your life. Remember, it's okay to prioritize your own well-being and surround yourself with people who uplift and support you.

☐

☐

☐

IDENTIFYING RELATIONSHIPS IN NEED OF REPAIR.

☐

☐

☐

REKINDLING OLD CONNECTIONS: THE PEOPLE YOU SHOULD REACH OUT TO TODAY.

☐ _____

☐ _____

☐ _____

MAKING TIME FOR THOSE WHO MATTER: THE PERSON YOU NEED TO VISIT ASAP.

☐ _____

☐ _____

☐ _____

SPREADING BIRTHDAY CHEER: THE IMPORTANCE OF SENDING HANDWRITTEN CARDS.

In today's fast-paced world, it can be easy to lose track of important dates such as birthdays. However, taking the time to send a thoughtful birthday card can make a world of difference and show your loved ones how much you care. So why not make a list of your friends' birthdays and commit to sending each of them a personalized note when their special day comes around? It doesn't have to be anything elaborate, just a simple message wishing them a happy birthday and letting them know how much they mean to you. With a little effort, you can brighten someone's day and strengthen your relationships with the important people in your life.

PRESERVING FAMILY LEGACY: THE TREASURED ITEMS YOU SHOULD SHARE WITH FUTURE GENERATIONS.

We all have treasured items that we hold dear, whether it's a set of fine china, expensive jewelry, or other valuable possessions. However, it's a shame to keep these items locked away and unused for fear of damaging or losing them. Instead, why not consider passing them down to loved ones who will appreciate them just as much as you do? Not only will you be able to share the joy of these items with others, but you'll also create lasting memories and strengthen your relationships.

And if possible, take pleasure in their enjoyment in person, whether it's sharing a meal with your good china or admiring your jewelry on someone you love. Life is too short to keep our treasures hidden away, so why not share them with those who matter most?

DONATE CLOTHES TO A THRIFT SHOP.

Cleaning out your closet and donating clothes to a thrift shop is a great way to declutter and make space for your favorite items. Plus, by donating to charity, you're helping those in need and supporting a good cause. On the other hand, if you love to shop, visiting a thrift shop can be a fun and inexpensive way to find unique items while also doing something good for the environment. You don't have to buy anything to enjoy the experience, browsing and discovering hidden treasures can be just as enjoyable. So whether you're donating or shopping, thrift shops offer a win-win situation for everyone involved.

GETTING ACTIVE AGAIN: REDISCOVERING PHYSICAL ACTIVITIES YOU'VE LOVED IN THE PAST.

PUSHING YOUR LIMITS: THE PHYSICAL ACTIVITIES YOU SHOULD TRY AT LEAST ONCE IN YOUR LIFE.

TAKE A DANCE CLASS AND LEARN A ROUTINE

If you're looking for a fun and exciting way to get moving, why not try taking a dance class and learning a routine? Whether you used to dance and want to revisit it or have always been a wallflower, dancing is a great way to challenge your brain and body while having fun. In fact, studies have shown that learning new dance moves can even have an anti-aging effect on the brain! With so many different styles and techniques to choose from, there's bound to be one that you'll enjoy.

SCALING NEW HEIGHTS: CONQUERING THREE OF THE HIGHEST PEAKS IN YOUR STATE.

If you're up for a physical challenge and love the great outdoors, why not research the ten highest peaks in your state and set a goal to climb three of them? Whether you prefer a slow and steady pace or a more intense workout, summiting a peak is a rewarding experience that offers incredible views and a sense of accomplishment. However, it's important to prepare accordingly and have the necessary supplies and equipment to ensure a safe and successful climb. Depending on the difficulty of the hike, you may need sturdy hiking boots, appropriate clothing, plenty of water and food, and even a map or compass. List the peaks you plan to climb here.

EXPAND YOUR COMFORT ZONE AND BOOST YOUR CONFIDENCE.

Are you feeling stuck in your routine and craving a little more excitement in your life? Why not try expanding your comfort zone? It may sound daunting, but it's actually quite simple. All you have to do is challenge yourself to do something that slightly scares you every day for a month. For example, if you're a bit shy, try saying hello to a stranger. By doing this, you'll gradually build your confidence and feel more comfortable in a variety of situations. And who knows? You may even discover a newfound courage to try even more things that once seemed scary. So why not give it a go and see where it takes you?

TRACKING YOUR EMOTIONAL WELL-BEING: THE BENEFITS OF KEEPING A MOOD DIARY FOR A WEEK.

Have you ever wondered what factors influence your mood and overall well-being? Keeping a mood diary for just seven days can help you discover insights about yourself and your daily routines. Simply track your mood each day and try to connect it with what you did or experienced that day. Did you feel particularly good on the days when you were spending time with loved ones or engaging in a favorite hobby? Take note of these patterns and try to incorporate more of these positive experiences into your life.

By doing so, you may find that your mood improves and you feel happier overall. Give it a try and see what you discover about yourself!

MONDAY
TUESDAY
WEDNESDAY
THURSDAY
FRIDAY
SATURDAY
SUNDAY

SPEND A WEEK FOCUSING ON THE GOOD THINGS IN LIFE.

Are you feeling a bit down or overwhelmed lately? One way to shift your perspective and boost your mood is to spend a week being grateful for all the good things in your life. We often take for granted the things that run smoothly or bring us joy, so taking deliberate notice of them can make a big difference. From the simple pleasures like a good cup of coffee or a refreshing night's sleep, to the more significant experiences like achieving a fitness goal or checking off a bucket list item, there's always something to be grateful for. By focusing on the good things that happen each day and writing down three things you're grateful for, you'll begin to see more positivity in your life and feel more content overall. So why not give it a try and see how it makes you feel?

I am grateful for...

MONDAY

1. _____

2. _____

3. _____

TUESDAY

1. _____

2. _____

3. _____

WEDNESDAY

1. _____

2. _____

3. _____

THURSDAY

1. _____

2. _____

3. _____

FRIDAY

1. _____

2. _____

3. _____

SATURDAY

1. _____

2. _____

3. _____

SUNDAY

1. _____

2. _____

3. _____

Healthy Skin, Happy You

Our skin is one of the most important organs of our body, but we often neglect to give it the care and attention it deserves. That's why it's important to do something nice for your skin twice a week for a month. It doesn't have to be anything extravagant – it could be as simple as doing a face mask at home, moisturizing your whole body if it's not something you regularly do, or giving yourself a relaxing manicure. By taking the time to care for your skin, you'll not only feel pampered and refreshed, but you'll also be doing your body a favor by keeping its largest organ healthy and glowing. So why not treat yourself to a little self-care and see how it makes you feel?

MEDITATE DAILY FOR TWO WEEKS

Have you ever felt overwhelmed or stressed out and wished you had a way to calm your mind and relax your body? Meditation may be just what you need. By taking just a few minutes each day to sit or lie down somewhere comfortable and concentrate on your breathing, you can improve your overall sense of well-being and reduce stress. Simply focus on taking slow, deep breaths in and out, and if your mind starts to wander, gently bring your attention back to your breath.

It may take a little practice, but over time you'll find that meditation becomes easier and more enjoyable. So why not try meditating daily for two weeks and see how it makes you feel? You may be surprised at the positive impact it can have on your mood and outlook.

GO ON A STARGAZING ADVENTURE.

Are you looking for a fun and inexpensive way to enjoy your retirement? Why not try going on a stargazing adventure? With just a little bit of planning, you can find the perfect spot in your state for a night of awe-inspiring stargazing. All you need is a clear night, a comfortable blanket, some drinks and snacks, and a sense of wonder. As you marvel at the beauty of the night sky, you'll feel a sense of peace and connection to the natural world around you. So why not take advantage of this simple yet magical experience and go on a stargazing adventure? You won't regret it!

GO FOR A WALK.

Do you want to improve your health and feel more energized? One of the easiest and most effective ways to do so is by walking more. And the best part is, it doesn't have to be a major commitment – every little bit of movement counts! You can start by parking farther away from your destination, taking an extra flight of stairs, or getting off the bus a stop early.

Even small tasks like cleaning your home yourself can add up to more physical activity throughout your day. By incorporating more walking into your routine, you'll not only improve your physical health, but also boost your mood and sense of well-being. So why not take a few extra steps each day and see how it makes you feel?

DEEPEN YOUR SPIRITUAL PRACTICE: BEGIN A PRAYER JOURNAL.

Consider starting a prayer journal to capture your deepest thoughts and intentions. Whether you communicate with God or simply send your desires out into the universe, a prayer journal can be a powerful tool for reflection and manifestation.

MANIFEST YOUR DESIRES WITH AFFIRMATIONS.

Affirmations are a powerful way to manifest your desires and bring positive changes into your life. Consider choosing one thing that you'd like to welcome into your life and spend a week repeating affirmations to yourself, either aloud or silently. As the mind and body are interconnected, the more you believe in something, the more likely it is to become a reality. If you're a retiree, some common affirmations may include "I'm grateful for the opportunity to spend time on my hobbies," "I maintain excellent health in retirement," or "I cherish the freedom to pursue my passions." Take some time to write down affirmations that resonate with you and repeat them daily to manifest the life you desire.

☐ _____

☐ _____

☐ _____

DO VOLUNTEER WORK.

Retirement is an ideal time to explore volunteering opportunities and give back to the community. Not only does it provide a sense of fulfillment and purpose, but it also helps you stay active and socially connected, which is crucial for your overall health and happiness. By offering your time and skills to those in need, you can make a positive impact on the world while also enriching your own life. So why not consider volunteering as a way to spend your retirement days and experience the joy of making a difference in the lives of others?

HELP SOMEONE IN NEED.

Retirement doesn't have to be expensive to be enjoyable. In fact, one of the most rewarding things you can do is to help someone in need. By offering your time and support, you can experience a sense of fulfillment and happiness that money can't buy. Whether it's visiting an elderly neighbor for a cup of coffee, doing the weekly groceries, performing a random act of kindness for a stranger, or sharing your wisdom and knowledge as a mentor or coach for the next generation, there are countless ways to give back and make a positive impact on others. So why not consider volunteering your time and talents to help someone else and experience the joy of making a difference?

DISCOVER YOUR LEGACY: SPEND AN HOUR REFLECTING ON THE POSITIVE IMPACT YOU'VE HAD ON OTHERS.

Take some time to reflect on your life and the impact you've had on others. Whether it's through your career accomplishments, charitable work, or simply being there for others as a compassionate listener, it's easy to lose sight of the positive difference you've made in the world. Set aside an hour to think about your proudest moments and reflect on the ways you've touched the lives of others. Perhaps you've helped a stranger get back on their feet, mentored a young person to success, or raised confident and capable children. Whatever your accomplishments may be, take the time to acknowledge them and feel proud of the positive impact you've had on the world. You may even be inspired to continue making a difference in new and meaningful ways.

GO TO A COMEDY SHOW

If there's a comedian you've been dying to see, why not book your tickets and make a night of it? Whether it's a well-known comic or a rising star, there's nothing quite like the energy and excitement of a live comedy performance. So go ahead and treat yourself to a night of fun and laughter.

So go ahead and treat yourself to a night of fun and laughter. If you have a particular comedian in mind, let me know and I'll help you find out if and when they're performing near you.

PRANK LOVED ONES

Retirement doesn't mean you have to be serious all the time. In fact, it's the perfect opportunity to let your playful side shine! Pranking your friends and loved ones can be a fun and lighthearted way to bring some laughter and joy into your relationships. Whether it's a surprise visit or a harmless joke, the element of surprise can create a rush of adrenaline and endorphins, leaving you both in stitches. Just make sure to keep it tame and tailored to your loved one's sense of humor. It's important to be respectful and avoid pranking strangers or anyone with anxiety, heightened stress, or a heart condition. So why not shake things up and surprise your loved ones with some lighthearted silliness?

DISCOVER NEW PASSIONS: EXPLORE HOBBIES YOU'VE ALWAYS WANTED TO TRY.

Retirement is the perfect time to explore new hobbies and interests. Whether you continue with them or not, the joy of discovering new activities is the point. Take some time to think about hobbies you've always wanted to try and make a list. Maybe you've always wanted to learn a new language, take up painting, or try your hand at gardening. Whatever it may be, write it down and commit to giving it a try. And if you have friends or family members who might be interested in joining you, add their names to the list. After all, trying new things is always more fun when you have someone to share the experience with. So why not take the leap and explore the endless possibilities of new hobbies and interests?

REDISCOVER YOUR PASSIONS: REVISIT HOBBIES YOU LOVED IN THE PAST.

Embrace the joy of rediscovery! Take a stroll down memory lane and recall those pastimes that once brought you immense pleasure. Now is the perfect opportunity to reignite the spark and rekindle your love for those hobbies you once cherished. So, seize the moment and pick your top three favorite activities that you'd like to relearn and restart. Write them down here and get ready to relive those moments of pure bliss!

UNLEASH YOUR CREATIVITY: BUILD YOUR OWN SCULPTURE.

Unleash your inner artist and let your creativity soar! Whether you choose to create a one-of-a-kind abstract masterpiece using everyday odds and ends or to sculpt something that holds a special place in your heart, now is the time to get started. So, grab your materials and dive into the wonderful world of sculpture-making. Who knows, you might just discover a hidden talent and create something truly breathtaking!

JOIN A LOCAL THEATER GROUP

Are you ready to unleash your inner performer and be part of a vibrant community of theater enthusiasts? Joining a local theater group can be an incredibly rewarding experience, whether you love to build sets, source props, put together costumes, or play an instrument in the live band or orchestra.

And if you're ready to take center stage and showcase your acting talents, the theater group is the perfect place to do so. So, why wait? Sign up today and let the magic of the theater unfold before your very eyes!

EXPAND YOUR HORIZONS: LEARN A NEW LANGUAGE AND CONNECT WITH DIFFERENT CULTURES.

Are you ready to expand your horizons and discover new cultures? Learning a new language is the perfect way to do just that! Thanks to modern technology, it's easier than ever to get started. Simply download a language-learning app like Duo Lingo, borrow a language book or CD from your local library, or purchase one from your nearby bookstore. With so many resources at your fingertips, there's no excuse not to start your language-learning journey today. So, why not take the first step and open the door to a whole new world of opportunities?

COMPLETE A DIY PROJECT.

Do you have any lingering home repairs that you've been putting off because you don't feel confident in your DIY skills? Don't let fear hold you back! With a bit of effort and some helpful tutorials, you can tackle those projects yourself and save money in the process. From painting a room to installing a floating shelf, there are plenty of tasks you can take on and learn from. Of course, it's important to prioritize safety and avoid taking on any electrical work that's beyond your expertise. But with some careful planning and a willingness to learn, you might surprise yourself with what you can accomplish.

Here are some project ideas to help you get started:
- Repaint a room to give it a fresh new look
- Install a floating shelf to add some stylish storage space
- Replace old, worn-out carpeting with new flooring

FEEL THE NEED FOR SPEED: EXPERIENCE THE THRILL OF DRIVING A RACE CAR.

Experience the thrill of a lifetime by signing up for a race car driving adventure at a nearby track. You can even make it a part of your next day trip or weekend getaway and add some excitement to your travel plans!

DYE YOUR HAIR A WILD COLOR OR CUT YOUR OWN HAIR

Are you feeling adventurous? Consider dying your hair a bold and vibrant color or even trying your hand at cutting your own hair! Don't worry too much about the results because after all, your hair will eventually grow back. So take the plunge and have some fun with your hair!

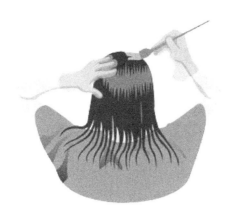

TRY SOMETHING NEW AND ATTEND AN UNCONVENTIONAL EVENT.

Step out of your comfort zone and try something new! Even if you think you wouldn't enjoy it, give an event or activity a chance that you wouldn't typically choose. Not a fan of ballet? Give it a try anyway! Don't see the appeal of monster truck rallies? Attend one and see for yourself! Unsure about farmers markets? Go check one out and you might be pleasantly surprised. You never know, you might find a new passion or appreciation for something you didn't expect!

UNLEASH YOUR POTENTIAL: TURN YOUR LIFETIME SKILLS INTO A THRIVING PART-TIME BUSINESS!

Retirement is a time to enjoy the fruits of your labor, but losing a steady income can be a concern. However, imagine having the freedom to turn your passions into profit without the pressure of relying on it for survival. You can let your creativity soar and utilize your existing skills to start a business that truly speaks to your heart. From selling handmade knitted items on Etsy to lending your green thumb to your neighbors' gardens, the possibilities are endless. You may even consider leveraging your artistic talents to design unique prints for on-demand sales or exploring your love for writing by publishing articles or books. Expand your horizons and brainstorm ideas that excite you. There's no limit to what you can achieve!

CONQUER A MARATHON AND ACHIEVE YOUR FITNESS GOALS!

Embarking on the journey to run a marathon demands unwavering dedication, both mentally and physically, not just on race day, but throughout the weeks and months of preparation leading up to it. It's an opportunity to push yourself beyond your limits and prove to yourself that you are capable of achieving incredible feats with the power of your mind and body.

With each step you take towards the finish line, you'll discover a newfound sense of strength, resilience, and determination that will inspire you to take on any challenge that comes your way. So, lace up your running shoes, set your sights on the finish line, and start your training journey today. The power to accomplish anything you set your mind to is within your reach.

PERFORM LIVE

Have you ever found yourself dreaming of the spotlight, whether it's through singing, slam poetry, or stand-up comedy? Well, here's your chance to make it a reality! Whether it's a grand stage or a small intimate one, don't let fear hold you back. Embrace your creativity and take a leap towards making your dreams a reality. The world is waiting for the magic that only you can bring to the stage. So, let your voice be heard, your words be felt, and your humor be appreciated. It's time to shine and show everyone what you're made of!

VISIT A WATER PARK

Why settle for a mundane day when you can make a splash and have a blast at a water park? Whether you're hanging out with your adult buddies or spending quality time with your grandkids, don't miss out on the excitement of zooming down thrilling water slides. So, ditch the sidelines and dive into the fun!

JET BOATING ADVENTURES AWAIT!

Look no further than jet boating! Experience the thrill of blasting past other boats and executing jaw-dropping 360° spins on the water. Just be sure to hold on tight as you embark on this unforgettable ride!

ENJOY AN ENCHANTING NIGHT AT THE OUTDOOR CINEMA!

Don't let the chill of the summer evening keep you from enjoying the great outdoors! Grab a cozy blanket, some warm clothes, and a comfortable camp chair, and get ready to bask in the natural beauty around you.

Feel the gentle breeze on your skin as you settle in for a fun and entertaining summertime movie under the stars. So, pack your essentials and get ready for an enchanting outdoor experience!

ESCAPE TO NATURE IN STYLE: EMBARK ON AN UNFORGETTABLE GLAMPING ADVENTURE!

If you're not up for roughing it out in the wilderness anymore, fear not! You can still relive the joys of camping by setting up a cozy tent in your own backyard. Roast some marshmallows over a crackling fire, and share some spine-tingling ghost stories with your grandkids - whether it's by the warmth of a real fire or through a spooky video playing on your iPad. Make your tent a haven of comfort and relaxation by filling it up with plush cushions and blankets. And if the great outdoors become too much to handle, you can always sneak back to your bed for a good night's rest!

PARTICIPATE IN A BEACH CLEAN UP.

Are you someone who values our planet and resides near the coast? Why not take part in a beach clean up and make a positive impact on the environment? It's an affordable and enjoyable retirement activity that can leave you feeling fulfilled.

Not living near a beach shouldn't stop you from getting involved! Consider joining a cleanup effort for a nearby forest or public park in your community. You'll be part of a movement to improve the environment and have the opportunity to meet fascinating new people along the way.

UNLEASH NON-STOP FUN AND LAUGHTER: DIVE INTO THE THRILL OF BOARD GAMES!

Why not blow the dust off your old board games and invite some friends over for a game night? Classic games like Monopoly and Pictionary are always a blast, but if you're looking for something fresh and exciting, my personal favorites are 30 Seconds, Rummikub, and Trivial Pursuit. So, gather some good company and get ready for an evening of laughter and fun!

Embrace the Cozy Charm of a Bonfire Night: Gather Around the Flames for Unforgettable Memories!

There's nothing quite like the warmth and magic of a bonfire. Gather some free wood from your backyard or a nearby forest, invite your friends to bring their favorite drinks and snacks, and don't forget to bring a guitar to sing the night away!

Watching the flames dance and hearing the soothing crackles of the fire can be incredibly relaxing, making it the perfect way to cap off a wonderful evening in retirement. So, light up that bonfire and enjoy the company of your loved ones as you bask in the glow of the fire.

PICK FRUIT.

Living in a fertile environment has its perks - you can actually pick your own fresh fruit! In retirement, consider checking out nearby farms or public parks where you can handpick delicious fruits such as strawberries, apples, or cherries.

Many farms offer the opportunity for visitors to pick their own fruit, which can be a fun and rewarding experience. Alternatively, you can also explore public parks that have fruit plants and enjoy the thrill of harvesting your own fresh produce. So, get outside, embrace nature, and savor the sweet taste of freshly picked fruit!

LEARN SOMETHING NEW WITH TOP FREE ONLINE CLASSES!

Retirement is a great time to continue your education by taking advantage of the many free online courses available. Whether you want to learn about a specific topic or enhance your existing skills, websites like Coursera and Udemy offer a plethora of courses to choose from.

These online platforms provide a wide variety of courses taught by industry experts and top universities, giving you the opportunity to learn at your own pace and on your own schedule. So, don't let retirement slow down your thirst for knowledge - browse through these websites and embark on a new learning adventure today!

VISIT GARAGE SALES AND LOOK FOR DEALS.

If you're looking to save some cash, consider browsing garage sales for fantastic bargains. It's not uncommon to find items that have been well taken care of and can be used for years to come without breaking the bank.

GET ACTIVE AND ENGAGE WITH YOUR COMMUNITY THROUGH SPORTS!

For sports lovers on a budget, community sports can be a great option. Watching a professional sports game can be costly, but community sports games are often more affordable and just as enjoyable to attend.

Alternatively, consider taking on a role as a coach for a local sports team. Many communities are in need of enthusiastic volunteers who are passionate about coaching and being involved in sports. Not only can this be a rewarding experience, but it can also be a great way to give back to your community.

TEACH YOURSELF HOW TO JUGGLE.

Retirement can be a great time to teach yourself new skills, and learning how to juggle is a fantastic and inexpensive option. Not only does it keep your mind sharp and boost your self-esteem, but it's also a fun way to impress family and friends at gatherings. The look on their faces will make the hours you put into it all worth it.

In addition to juggling, there are plenty of other affordable ways to keep yourself challenged and occupied in retirement. Why not try your hand at knitting? Or learn a new card or magic trick to impress your loved ones.

You could even master the cup song to delight your grandchildren or teach your dog a new trick. The possibilities are endless!

BUILDING BRIDGES, ONE NEIGHBOR AT A TIME: DISCOVER THE JOYS OF MEETING AND CONNECTING WITH YOUR COMMUNITY!

If you haven't had the chance to meet your new neighbors or get to know your existing ones, why not take the initiative to reach out to them? A simple introduction can go a long way in building strong relationships with those around you.

Consider dropping by with a homemade pie or offering your services to lend a hand. After all, having good neighbors can be just as valuable as having close friends. You might even think about organizing a neighborhood barbecue or get-together to strengthen connections and foster a sense of community. Taking the time to connect with your neighbors can lead to lasting friendships and a happier, more fulfilling life.

SET A NEW GOAL IN LIFE.

Setting goals is a crucial aspect of personal growth and development. Doing so allows you to move forward, challenge yourself, and maintain a sense of purpose and direction in life.

As Albert Einstein famously stated, "Life is like riding a bicycle. To keep your balance, you must keep moving." So, take a moment to grab a pen and paper and jot down a new life goal. Research has shown that writing down your goals increases your chances of achieving them, so why not give it a try? By setting goals, you can give yourself something to work towards, stay motivated, and ultimately live a more fulfilling life.

DISCOVER THE ART OF PHOTOGRAPHY WITH JUST YOUR PHONE.

Embark on a new hobby of photography with your trusty smartphone! Believe it or not, your phone can capture stunning photos that you can enjoy in your retirement. Not only is it a fun and fulfilling activity, but it's also budget-friendly.

With a plethora of free photo editing apps like Snapseed, Prisma Photo Editor, and VSCO, you can elevate your photos to a whole new level. And if you're looking to improve your skills, YouTube is a treasure trove of amazing tutorials that can guide you on how to capture and edit the best photos with your phone.

CREATE A SCRAPBOOK FROM OLD PICTURES.

As we age, we often accumulate a treasure trove of old photographs that hold cherished memories. Instead of letting them gather dust in a box, why not turn them into a beautiful scrapbook or photo book? Not only is it a fun and creative activity, but it's also a budget-friendly way to spend a cozy day indoors when the weather outside is less than ideal. So, grab a cup of tea and relive your favorite moments as you craft a keepsake that will be treasured for years to come.

PRACTICE MEDITATION.

Retirement is a time to enjoy life to the fullest, but it's not always stress-free. That's why incorporating meditation into your daily routine can be incredibly beneficial. Not only does it promote a sense of calm and happiness, but it can also reduce stress and anxiety. In fact, numerous studies have shown that regular meditation practice can have science-based benefits for emotional health, such as reducing stress levels and controlling anxiety. So, why not give it a try and see how it can positively impact your retirement years?

UNLEASH THE THRILL OF TREASURE HUNTING: GO MAGNET FISHING AND DISCOVER HIDDEN GEMS IN THE WATER!

This simple activity involves attaching a magnet to a fishing line and casting it into nearby rivers and lakes to see what treasures you can discover. From old coins and jewelry to discarded tools and even historical artifacts, the possibilities are endless. However, it's important to note that due to its growing popularity, magnet fishing may not be allowed in all areas. So, be sure to check the rules and regulations in your region and invest in a quality magnet fishing kit for an unforgettable adventure. Who knows? You may just uncover a hidden treasure!

CREATE A FAMILY TREE.

Do you ever wonder about your family's history and where your ancestors came from? Retirement is the perfect time to dive into your past and create a family tree. With the help of websites, you can uncover a wealth of information about your lineage. If your family has been in the area for a long time, your local library can also be a valuable resource. They can help you track down centuries-old birth certificates and other records to fill in the gaps of your family's story. But don't forget to also ask within your family!

The oldest living members can provide valuable insights and memories about their parents, cousins, aunts, uncles, and grandparents. By piecing together your family's history, you can create a rich and meaningful legacy for generations to come.

CHERISH THE JOY OF GRANDPARENTING: SPEND QUALITY TIME WITH YOUR GRANDCHILDREN AND CREATE LASTING MEMORIES!

They say that being a grandparent is one of life's greatest joys, and what better way to spend your retirement days than by babysitting your beloved grandchildren? If you don't see your grandkids as often as you'd like, why not ask if you can be more involved? You could become their go-to babysitter and spend quality time with them while also giving their parents a much-needed break.

But what if you don't have grandchildren or they live far away? Don't worry, there are still plenty of opportunities to share your love and care with other children. Consider babysitting kids from your neighborhood or friends' circle, or become a foster grandparent for kids who don't have grandparents in their lives. Not only will you be providing support and care for little ones who need it, but you'll also be filling your days with joy and purpose.

DISCOVER THE POWER OF SELF-REFLECTION: START JOURNALING AND UNLEASH YOUR INNERMOST THOUGHTS AND EMOTIONS!

Journaling is a remarkably affordable form of therapy that requires nothing more than a journal, a pen, and a few minutes of your time each day. Not only is it cost-effective, but it also has a host of incredible benefits for managing stress and improving overall mental health.

In fact, did you know that journaling is one of the most effective stress management tools available? By engaging in expressive writing, you can enhance your mental clarity, solve problems more effectively, and boost your focus.

The benefits of journaling are numerous and powerful. Here are just a few ways that it can positively impact your health:

1. Reduces stress levels
2. Improves immune function
3. Keeps your memory sharp
4. It boosts your mood
5. Strengthens emotional functions

UNLOCK SAVINGS AT EVERY TURN: GO ON A COUPON SCAVENGER HUNT AND SCORE BIG ON YOUR NEXT SHOPPING SPREE!

Embark on an exciting coupon scavenger hunt and discover amazing deals on products you frequently buy. By taking advantage of valuable discounts, you can save a significant amount of money and enjoy great savings.

Start your hunt by scouring through your local newspapers and magazines to locate coupons that appeal to you. You can also reach out to your friends and neighbors and ask if they have any unused coupons they're willing to share.

With a little bit of effort, you can amass a collection of fantastic coupons that will help you save big on your everyday purchases. So gear up for an adventure and uncover all the amazing deals that are just waiting for you!

GET INTO THE SPOOKY SPIRIT: DRESS UP YOUR HOUSE OR YOURSELF FOR HALLOWEEN AND CREATE A HAUNTINGLY MEMORABLE EXPERIENCE!

When was the last time you went all out for Halloween? Have you ever given candy to children at your doorstep or volunteered to take your loved ones' children trick-or-treating so that their parents can have a night to themselves?

This Halloween, why not immerse yourself in the community and enjoy the festivities with your neighbors? Take advantage of this spooky night and get to know some of your neighbors that you may not have met yet.

As the streets fill with families enjoying each other's company, embrace the fun and excitement of this holiday. So don't miss out on the opportunity to be a part of the festivities and make new connections with those around you.

HOST A FRIENDS-GIVING PARTY

You don't have to plan a fancy gathering to spend quality time with your loved ones who you don't usually see during the busy holiday season. Consider inviting them over for a casual afternoon or evening at home, or even going out somewhere special to celebrate the meaningful relationships you share with each other.

HAVE A FOOD FIGHT AND INDULGE IN MESSY, DELICIOUS FUN WITH YOUR LOVED ONES!

Gather your closest friends, pick out some deliciously indulgent foods like ooey, gooey cheeses and sauces, and get ready to have some messy fun! Whether you're experimenting with different flours or mixing up unique sauces, the possibilities are endless. So grab your bucket list buddies and let the culinary battle begin!

JUMP IN THE MUD

Get ready to embrace your inner child and jump into the mud! Just remember to keep a hose nearby to rinse off before heading back inside. It's a fun and messy way to let loose and enjoy the great outdoors without worrying about getting a little dirty. So go ahead, take the plunge, and have some muddy fun!

LET THE SNOW GAMES BEGIN!

Living in a snowy climate can mean a lot of work when heavy snowfall hits. But instead of seeing it as a burden, why not add some fun and unexpected silliness to your day? Challenge your friends, family, or even strangers to a snowball fight! It's a great way to not only lighten the mood but also get some exercise and fresh air. So, next time the snow starts falling, grab some gloves and embrace your inner child with a playful snowball fight.

MAKE A SNOWMAN

When was the last time you built a snowman out of freshly fallen snow? Take a refreshing trip down memory lane and create a new friend out of snow! Not only is building a snowman a fun and nostalgic activity, but it's also a great way to get outside and enjoy the winter weather. So, gather some sticks and rocks for the eyes and buttons, and let your creativity run wild as you craft a unique and charming snowman. It's the perfect way to make new memories and embrace the winter season.

SPREAD JOY AND DELICIOUSNESS: HOST A CHRISTMAS COOKIE DECORATING PARTY AND CREATE SWEET MEMORIES WITH YOUR LOVED ONES!

After a successful (or even unsuccessful) baking session with friends or family, surprise them all with a delicious treat you've prepared yourself - mulled wine or eggnog! As the sun sets, cozy up in comfy clothes in front of a warm fire with a furry friend nearby and share life stories over freshly baked cookies. It's the perfect way to unwind and enjoy the company of loved ones while indulging in some homemade treats and heartwarming conversation. So, grab your favorite mug and let the good times roll!

TREAT YOURSELF TO BLISSFUL RELAXATION: CREATE YOUR OWN AT-HOME SPA DAY AND INDULGE IN PURE PAMPERING!

When the weather outside is miserable, why not treat yourself to a cozy day indoors? Pamper yourself with a homemade face mask, paint your nails, and take some deep, relaxing breaths. Sip on some champagne and indulge in some much-needed self-care. It's the perfect way to recharge and rejuvenate while enjoying some well-deserved relaxation. So, put on your comfiest clothes, light some candles, and let the pampering begin!

HAVE A CHRISTMAS MOVIE MARATHON

Get into the holiday spirit by snuggling up under a cozy blanket and indulging in some delightfully cheesy Christmas movies. Embrace the sickly sweetness of these guilty pleasures and let yourself fully immerse in the festive atmosphere. Whether you prefer classic movies or newer releases, there's something for everyone. So, grab some popcorn, turn on the twinkling lights, and let the holiday cheer wash over you. It's the perfect way to spend a cozy day or night at home.

HOST A TACKY CHRISTMAS SWEATER PARTY AND SPREAD CHEER WITH YOUR LOVED ONES!

Start a new annual holiday tradition by hosting a festive gathering with party games and a "worst sweater" contest. Invite a mix of loved ones, acquaintances you'd like to get to know better, and friends who may not have met each other yet. If you enjoy spending time with all of these people, chances are they'll enjoy each other's company too! It's a great way to bring people together and create new connections while having some lighthearted fun. So, break out the board games, whip up some festive snacks, and let the holiday festivities begin!

NATURE'S SERENITY AWAITS: TAKE A STROLL IN THE PARK AND IMMERSE YOURSELF IN THE BEAUTY OF BLOOMING FLOWERS!

Slow down and take a moment to appreciate the beauty of nature around you. Take the time to observe the intricacies of flowers and leaves, and watch as butterflies and bees pollinate them. Notice all the life that exists around you and take in the wonders of the natural world. It's a great way to embrace mindfulness and find peace in the present moment. So, next time you're out for a walk or spending time in nature, take a deep breath and let yourself fully immerse in the beauty around you.

UNLEASH YOUR INNER ACTOR: HOST A BACKYARD PLAY WITH THE CHILDREN IN YOUR LIFE AND CREATE AN UNFORGETTABLE PERFORMANCE!

Get creative and put on a show with your kids or friends! Write your own story or perform a rendition of a favorite tale. Dress up in costumes, choreograph some silly moves, and set up chairs outside for your audience. It's the perfect way to let your imagination run wild and have some fun with the people you love. So, grab some props, rehearse your lines, and let the show begin! Whether it's a comedy, drama, or musical, the only limit is your creativity.

EMBARK ON A TASTY ADVENTURE: SAVOR THE FLAVORS OF THE WORLD AT AN INTERNATIONAL FOOD FESTIVAL AND BROADEN YOUR CULINARY HORIZONS!

Take a leisurely stroll through a farmers' market or food festival and indulge in the sights and smells of all the delicious offerings. Wander through the stalls, taking in the colorful displays and chatting with the vendors. Immerse yourself in the bustling atmosphere and maybe even discover your new favorite food to cook at home. It's a great way to support local businesses and farmers while also savoring the flavors of the season. So, grab a tote bag and some cash, and let your taste buds guide you through the market.

Festival:

_____

Cuisine:

_____

Favorite dish:

_____

STEP INTO A WORLD OF WONDER: IMMERSE YOURSELF IN ART, HISTORY, AND CULTURE AT MUSEUMS NEAR YOU!

Visiting museums can be a fascinating and healthy activity for seniors, as recent research shows that those who visit museums regularly report better mental and physical health than those who don't. Moreover, seniors who create their own art or attend museums have lower rates of hypertension and better cognitive and physical functioning than those who don't. In these studies, cognitive and physical health were measured through self-reported memory, physical activity limitations, and rates of hypertension and blood pressure.

While there has been an increase in seniors' attendance at museums, not all seniors have access to these cultural venues. For those with physical or cognitive limitations or limited access to museums, it's important to seek out local opportunities to explore art, such as smaller exhibits or community events. By experiencing the beauty and creativity of art, seniors can enhance their well-being and quality of life. So, whether it's a large museum or a local art exhibit, seniors are encouraged to take advantage of these opportunities to boost their physical and mental health.

HIT THE GREENS AND UNWIND: EXPERIENCE THE JOY OF GOLFING AND MASTER YOUR SWING FOR A DAY OF FUN AND RELAXATION!

Golfing is an excellent hobby for seniors, as it promotes socialization and has numerous health benefits. Seniors who take up golfing often find it to be an enjoyable and rewarding activity that improves their concentration and overall quality of life. Studies have suggested that playing golf can enhance seniors' walking and standing abilities, strength, balance, and cognitive function, as it requires players to pay attention and remember their scores.

Golf also offers the opportunity for friendly competition with friends and oneself, as players can continually work to improve their game and beat their previous scores. Whether it's a relaxing day on the course or a challenging round with friends, golfing is a wonderful way for seniors to stay active and engaged in life. So, grab your clubs and hit the links for some fun and healthy outdoor activity.

EXPAND YOUR MIND AND CHALLENGE YOUR THINKING: EMBARK ON A JOURNEY OF DISCOVERY WITH THE FASCINATING STUDY OF PHILOSOPHY!

Exploring philosophy can be an engaging and thought-provoking hobby for seniors looking to ponder life's bigger questions. By studying various philosophical schools of thought, seniors can develop their critical thinking and reasoning skills while uncovering new insights and beliefs about the purpose of their journey. Philosophy can also be a great conversation starter and a way to connect with others who share similar interests.

There are numerous books and resources available for seniors looking to dive into philosophy and explore different perspectives on the origins of life. As they delve deeper into this fascinating topic, they may discover new truths and insights that can enrich their lives and deepen their understanding of the world around them. So, whether you're a lifelong learner or just looking for a new hobby, exploring philosophy is a great way to keep your mind engaged and your curiosity alive.

EMPOWER YOURSELF WITH THE ULTIMATE SELF-DEFENSE TOOL: LEARN TO PROTECT YOURSELF AND GAIN PEACE OF MIND WITH SELF-DEFENSE CLASSES!

It's unfortunate that criminal activity against seniors is on the rise, making it important for them to feel confident in their ability to defend themselves in case of an emergency. Learning self-defense is a great way for seniors to not only improve their physical fitness but also increase their awareness of their surroundings and prevent an attack from happening.

Self-defense training can offer a wide range of physical benefits, including improved balance, flexibility, coordination, strength, and endurance. By practicing self-defense techniques, seniors can develop the skills and confidence needed to escape threats and protect themselves and their loved ones. Additionally, self-defense training can help seniors make safer choices and avoid potentially dangerous situations.

It's important to note that self-defense training should be tailored to the individual's physical abilities and limitations. Seniors should consult with their healthcare provider before starting any new physical activity to ensure it's safe for them. With proper training and practice, self-defense can be a valuable tool for seniors to stay safe and confident in their daily lives.

CHESS

Chess is an excellent game for seniors to play, whether alone or with others. With the availability of virtual players and online partners, seniors can play chess anytime and from anywhere in the world. This game of strategy can help seniors maintain their cognitive health and keep their minds active.

Playing chess is a great way to exercise problem-solving, memory, and analytical skills as seniors try to make the most strategic decisions to win the game. With endless winning strategies to learn, chess offers seniors an ongoing challenge that can help improve cognitive function and keep the mind sharp. Focusing on the game can also provide a welcomed escape from everyday problems as seniors try to plan several moves ahead and anticipate their opponent's next move.

Whether played online or in-person, chess is a fun and engaging way for seniors to stay mentally active and socially connected. So, whether you're a seasoned player or just starting out, grab a board or log in to your computer and challenge yourself to a game of chess.

PLAY VIDEO GAMES

Playing healthy video games in moderation can be a great way to keep yourself entertained and mentally engaged. Whether playing alone or with friends and family, video games offer a variety of options to suit different interests and abilities.

Games like Wii Sports can provide a fun way to get some exercise and stay energized, while games like Super Mario 3D World can stimulate the imagination and boost memory retention. Taking care of the hippocampus, a key part of the brain responsible for memory, can help lower the risk of Alzheimer's and other serious illnesses.

Other popular video games like World of Warcraft, Minecraft, and Animal Crossing: New Leaf offer endless hours of fun and entertainment, while mobile games like Candy Crush, Wordscapes, Two Dots, Words with Friends, and Lexulous can be played on-the-go and are often difficult to put down.

It's important to remember that playing video games can be addictive, so it's essential to take breaks when necessary. Additionally, seniors should consult with their healthcare provider before starting any new physical activity, including video games, to ensure it's safe for them. With moderation and proper precautions, video games can be a fun and engaging way for seniors to stay active and mentally sharp.

SHELLING

Shelling is a popular hobby that can be both relaxing and rewarding for seniors. While exploring the beach, shelling enthusiasts can learn to identify different types of shells and other objects that have washed ashore, such as shark teeth, driftwood, and sea glass. This hobby offers the opportunity to connect with nature, enjoy the beautiful scenery, and discover new treasures.

Once a collection of shells and other objects has been amassed, seniors can use their findings to create beautiful arts and crafts projects, decorate their homes, or take vivid photos before returning the shells back to nature. Incorporating shells into various art forms can be a creative and fulfilling way to showcase their beauty and uniqueness.

Shelling can also be a social activity, as seniors can join shelling groups or clubs to meet others who share their interests. These groups often organize shelling trips and beach cleanups, which can be a great way to connect with others and give back to the environment.

Overall, shelling is a fun and engaging hobby that offers a variety of benefits for seniors, including the opportunity to connect with nature, learn new skills, and socialize with others who share their interests.

BOWLING

Although bowling may not be a profound experience, it can certainly bring a lot of joy. What's more, it has numerous health benefits, such as improving blood flow, increasing bone density, and reducing the risk of diabetes, heart disease, and stroke. In fact, maintaining good health can be a great reason to hit the bowling alley. Whether you prefer to bowl alone or with a group of friends, you're almost guaranteed to have a blast. Not only will you enhance your cognitive abilities, but you'll also get to spend quality time with your loved ones. And if you become hooked on this popular pastime, you can even bring your own ball next time!

CARE FOR A PET

Loneliness and depression are common issues among seniors, but having a pet can provide much-needed companionship and encourage physical activity. Dogs, in particular, are great companions as they can adjust their schedule to match yours, and smaller breeds are easy to take with you on trips. In addition to the emotional benefits, caring for a pet can help seniors maintain a daily routine and provide a sense of purpose. Taking care of a pet may seem like a big responsibility, but the simple tasks of feeding and walking a dog can give structure and meaning to a senior's day. Finally, pet ownership can also help seniors stay connected to the outside world, by attending vet appointments, grooming sessions, and joining other dog owners for walks.

BIRD WATCHING

For those who used to enjoy hiking and camping but now want a more leisurely outdoor experience, bird watching is a fantastic option. It allows retirees to enjoy the great outdoors at their own pace while still being mindful of their surroundings. Whether you prefer to visit your favorite hiking spots or stay closer to home, bird watching can be a fascinating hobby for anyone. You can choose to bird watch solo or join a group for some socializing.

Watching birds in their natural habitats offers a unique way to connect with nature and appreciate the local ecosystems. With their different calls, feathers, colors, and behaviors, birds provide endless opportunities for observation and learning. Plus, this hobby can encourage you to pay more attention to other aspects of nature too.

Finally, bird watching is an excellent activity for seniors as it helps to exercise reflexes while trying to identify different bird species. It's a wonderful way to stay engaged with nature and get some exercise while still enjoying a relaxing outdoor experience.

UNLEASH YOUR INNER COMPETITOR: HAVE FUN AND CHALLENGE YOURSELF WITH AN ARRAY OF SOLO GAMES!

Playing games is a fantastic way for seniors to exercise their minds and improve their mental health, even when they're playing alone. Crossword puzzles, jigsaw puzzles, and Sudoku are all great examples of games that can provide significant benefits.

Crossword puzzles, in particular, have been a favorite among seniors for years. They are excellent for keeping the mind sharp and improving memory, as they require the use of one's vocabulary and knowledge to solve clues. These puzzles can be found in newspapers, magazines, and online, making them easily accessible.

Jigsaw puzzles, on the other hand, require focused attention and provide numerous benefits, including improving problem-solving skills, attention span, short-term memory, and reducing stress levels. By engaging both sides of the brain, jigsaw puzzles offer an excellent mental workout that can help seniors stay sharp and focused.

Sudoku is another game that offers similar benefits, including improved logic, concentration, a healthy mindset, reduced stress levels, and a sense of accomplishment.

Aside from their mental health benefits, these games are also affordable and accessible, making them a great way for seniors to stay engaged and entertained.

PASS ON YOUR KNOWLEDGE AND INSPIRE OTHERS: DISCOVER THE JOY OF TEACHING AND MAKE A POSITIVE IMPACT IN YOUR COMMUNITY!

Before you retired, what did you do for work? Or perhaps, what has been your lifelong passion? Whatever knowledge you've accumulated over the years, you have the power to share it with others who are just starting out.

There are numerous adult education programs that hire part-time instructors to teach evening courses on various hobbies such as cooking, learning a new language, and sewing. Teaching a subject that you're truly passionate about can be incredibly rewarding, and it can also provide you with some extra income.

UNLEASH YOUR CREATIVITY AND PRECISION: LEARN THE ART OF ORIGAMI AND TURN ORDINARY PAPER INTO EXTRAORDINARY WORKS OF ART!

Origami is a beautiful type of art that requires focus, dexterity, and fine motor skills. This inexpensive hobby can help you create stunning decorations for your home or gifts like cards and more. Despite its intricate appearance, origami is easy to learn and can be an excellent way to express your creativity and stay engaged.

In addition, research suggests that origami can have significant benefits for seniors, including improving cognitive skills and focus. It stimulates the brain as you create shapes by folding paper, making it an excellent activity for senior centers. Specific modified origami figures are even taught to those suffering from Alzheimer's to help improve their mental acuity and cognitive skills.

Origami is also a relaxing activity that can boost self-esteem and provide a sense of satisfaction after creating new shapes. Moreover, it can enhance a person's 3D comprehension skills, imagination, and motivation to create new designs. All you need is paper, and you can do it anywhere, alone or with your loved ones.

Seniors can even teach their grandchildren how to make various shapes like birds, fish, frogs, and flowers beyond the usual paper airplanes.

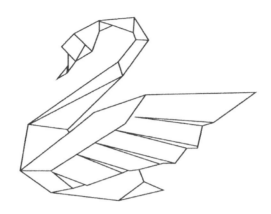

BECOME A TOUR GUIDE

Volunteering as a tour guide can be a fantastic way to indulge your love of history and culture while also giving back to your community. Not only will you have the opportunity to learn more about fascinating places and artifacts, but you'll also get to share your knowledge and enthusiasm with others. Whether you're interested in becoming a room guide, conservation assistant, or storyteller, there are a variety of roles available through organizations like the National Trust and others. By volunteering as a tour guide, you'll not only satisfy your own curiosity and passion, but you'll also help others to appreciate and value the rich heritage.

BECOME AN ONLINE GAMER

When it comes to keeping your mind sharp and active, puzzles and games have long been touted as a great way to exercise your brain. And with the rise of online gaming, seniors are finding even more ways to challenge themselves and connect with others. Websites like Chess.com, TheJigsawPuzzles.com, Lexulous.com (Scrabble), and Facebook.com/Games offer a range of options for puzzle enthusiasts and gamers alike, providing opportunities to connect with people from all over the world and engage in friendly competition. But don't limit yourself to traditional games - there's no reason why seniors can't hold their own in popular games like World of Warcraft or Fortnite. So why not give online gaming a try? Not only will you have fun and stay mentally sharp, but you might just surprise yourself by discovering a new passion or talent.

GROW YOUR FRIENDSHIP GROUP

Retirement is a great time to expand your social circle and get to know a wider range of people, including those from different age groups. By making friends with people of all ages, you'll have the opportunity to learn new things, experience different perspectives, and keep your mind open and engaged. In addition to enjoying the company of your peers, consider signing up for a pen pal scheme like Post-pals, which connects you with seriously ill children who could use a bit of cheer and encouragement. By sending letters, cards, and gifts, you'll not only brighten their day, but you'll also benefit from the satisfaction of making a positive difference in someone else's life. So why not take the time to reach out and make new connections? You never know what kind of wonderful experiences and friendships might be waiting for you.

LEARN TO PLAY AN INSTRUMENT: LEARN ANYTHING!

Learning to play a musical instrument can be a rewarding and fulfilling pursuit, regardless of whether you consider yourself musically inclined or not. With so many different instruments to choose from, including piano, guitar, banjo, and voice, there's sure to be one that resonates with you. Not only can playing music be a source of joy and enrichment, but it's also a pursuit that never truly ends - even the most accomplished musicians continue to practice and learn throughout their lives. By challenging yourself to learn a new skill, you'll also be supporting your brain health and cognitive function, keeping your mind sharp and active. So why not pick up an instrument and start exploring the world of music? You might just discover a new passion that brings you a lifetime of enjoyment and fulfillment.

KEEP UP WITH TECHNOLOGY

As the world becomes increasingly reliant on technology, it's important for seniors to stay up-to-date and comfortable with the latest gadgets and tools. While it can be intimidating to navigate new technologies, there are many benefits to embracing them. From staying connected with loved ones through social media and video calls, to accessing online services and resources, technology can enhance your quality of life and give you greater independence. By taking the time to learn about new technologies and practice using them, you'll gain the skills and confidence to keep up with the rapidly changing digital landscape. So don't be afraid to dive in and explore the world of technology - you might just discover new ways to stay engaged, connected, and fulfilled in your retirement years.

FIND A PART-TIME JOB

As a senior, you may not always require additional income, but having some extra money in your pocket can allow you to indulge in things you may not have considered before. You can explore various internet job sites to find companies that are seeking individuals willing to work a few hours a week, providing you with an opportunity to earn some extra spending cash.

CONCLUSION

retirement is a time to enjoy the fruits of your labor and explore new opportunities. Whether it's traveling to new destinations, learning a new hobby, or spending time with loved ones, there are countless fun things to do in retirement. By staying active, engaged, and curious, retirees can make the most of their time and create lasting memories. So go ahead and embrace all the exciting possibilities that retirement has to offer!

Made in the USA
Las Vegas, NV
16 December 2023

83007424R00049